HAL LEONARD
STUDENT
PIANO
LIBRARY

More Popular Piano Solos

Complements All Piano Methods

Table of Contents

	Page No.	CD Track	GM Disk Track
Part Of Your World from Walt Disney's THE LITTLE MERMAID	2	1	1
God Help The Outcasts from Walt Disney's THE HUNCHBACK OF NOTRE DAME	4	3	2
I Whistle A Happy Tune from THE KING AND I	6	5	3
Sesame Street Theme	8	7	4
Stand By Me featured in the Motion Picture STAND BY ME	10	9	5
Tomorrow from the Musical Production ANNIE	13	11	6
Once Upon A Dream from Walt Disney's SLEEPING BEAUTY	16	13	7
A Dream Is A Wish Your Heart Makes from Walt Disney's CINDERELLA	19	15	8
Go The Distance from Walt Disney Pictures' HERCULES	22	17	9
What A Wonderful World	26	19	10
Climb Ev'ry Mountain from THE SOUND OF MUSIC	29	21	11
The Bare Necessities from Walt Disney's THE JUNGLE BOOK	32	23	12

More Popular Piano Solos Level 3 is designed for use with the third book of any piano method.

Concepts in *More Popular Piano Solos Level 3*:

Range

Symbols

pp, *p*, *mp*, *mf*, *f*, *ff*, ♯, ♭, ♮, *ritard*, *a tempo*,

D.S. al Fine, To Coda ⊕, *8va, loco,* ⌒

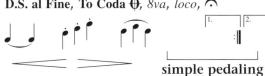

simple pedaling

Rhythm

time signatures: $\frac{4}{4}$, $\frac{3}{4}$

swing eighths

Intervals

2nd, 3rd, 4th, 5th, 6th
melodic and harmonic

ISBN 0-634-03569-X

HAL•LEONARD
CORPORATION

7777 W. BLUEMOUND RD. P.O. BOX 13819 MILWAUKEE, WI 53213

Visit Hal Leonard Online at
www.halleonard.com

6-14-05

Part Of Your World

from Walt Disney's THE LITTLE MERMAID

Lyrics by Howard Ashman
Music by Alan Menken
Arranged by Mona Rejino

Moderately bright (♩ = 112)

I wan-na be where the peo-ple are.
I wan-na see, wan-na see 'em danc-in',
walk-in' a-round on those, what-d-ya call 'em, oh feet.
Flip-pin' your fins you don't get too far. Legs are re-quired __ for

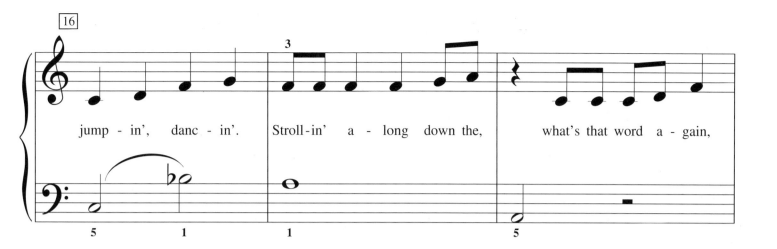

jump - in', danc - in'. Stroll-in' a - long down the, what's that word a - gain,

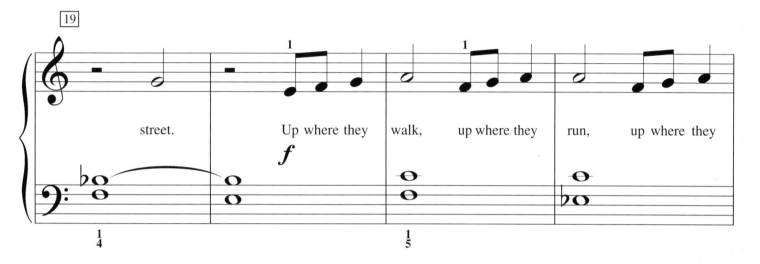

street. Up where they walk, up where they run, up where they

stay all day in the sun. Wan - der - in' free, wish I could

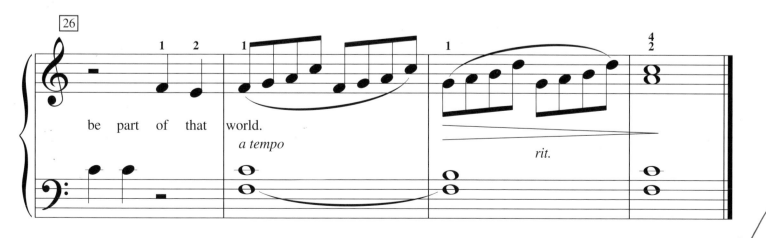

be part of that world.

God Help The Outcasts

from Walt Disney's THE HUNCHBACK OF NOTRE DAME

Music by Alan Menken
Lyrics by Stephen Schwartz
Arranged by Phillip Keveren

look   to   You   still.
poor   and   down-   trod.

God   help   the   out - casts   or
I   thought   we   all   were   the

no - bod - y   will.
chil - dren   of

1.

p

God. _____

God   help   the   out - casts,

rit.

chil - dren   of   God.

p   *a tempo*

rit.

pp

I Whistle A Happy Tune

from THE KING AND I

Lyrics by Oscar Hammerstein II
Music by Richard Rodgers
Arranged by Fred Kern

Moderately, in 'two' (♩ = 84)

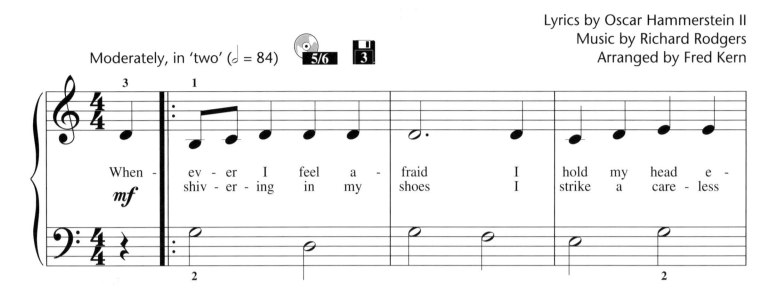

When - ev - er I feel a - fraid I hold my head e -
shiv - er - ing in my shoes I strike a care - less

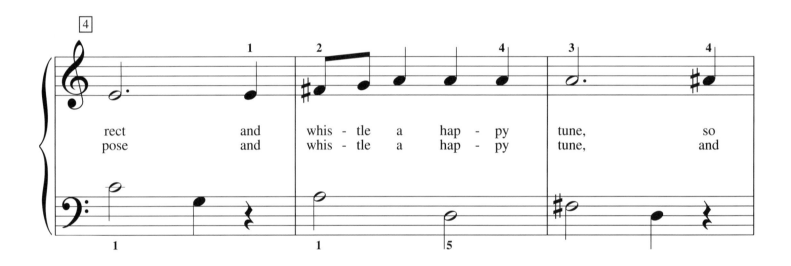

rect and whis - tle a hap - py tune, so
pose and whis - tle a hap - py tune, and

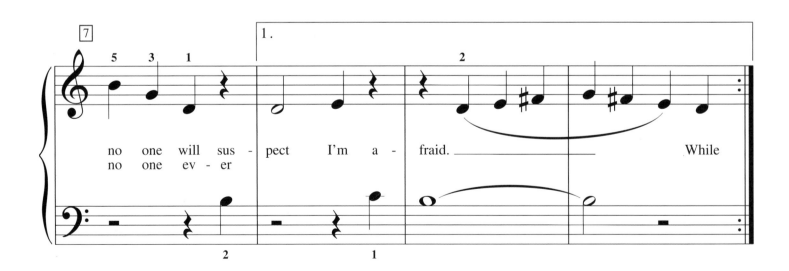

no one will sus - pect I'm a - fraid. While
no one ev - er

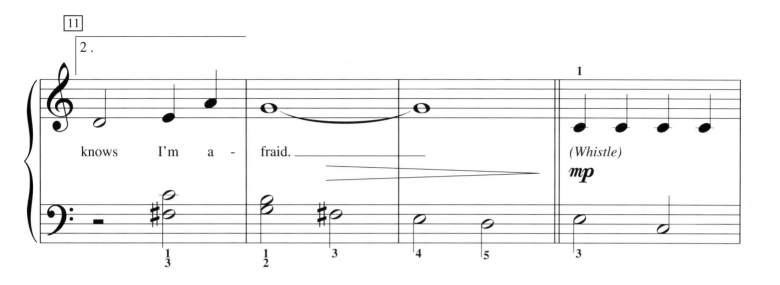

knows   I'm a - fraid. _____ (Whistle)

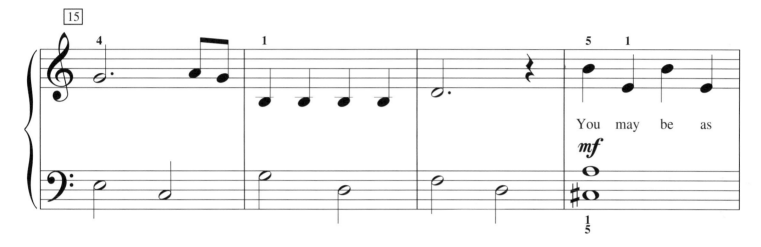

You   may   be   as

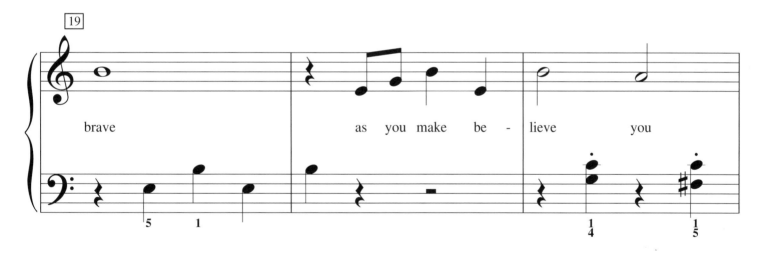

brave   as you make be - lieve   you

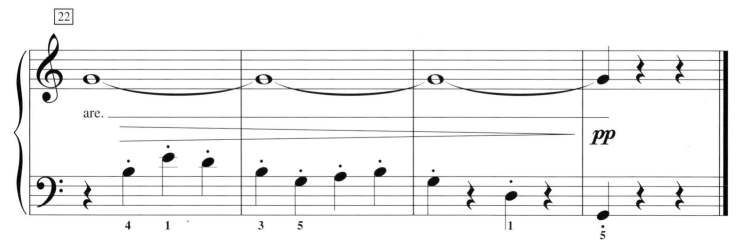

are. _____

Sesame Street Theme

Words by Bruce Hart, Jon Stone and Joe Raposo
Music by Joe Raposo
Arranged by Phillip Keveren

Stand By Me

featured in the Motion Picture STAND BY ME

Words and Music by Ben E. King,
Jerry Leiber and Mike Stoller
Arranged by Phillip Keveren

Steady Rock beat (♩ = 100)

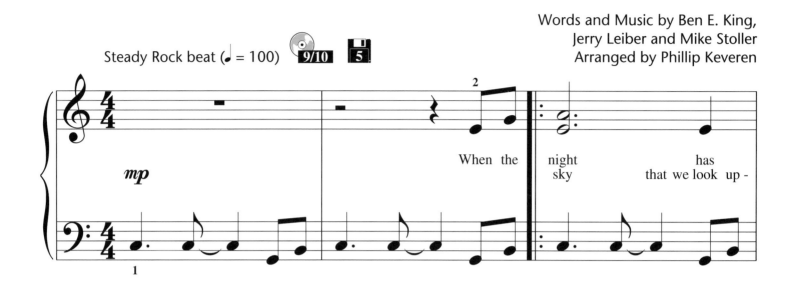

When the night sky has that we look up-

come on and the land is dark, and the
on should tum-ble and fall or the

moon _____ is the on - ly _____ light we'll see, _____
moun - tain _____ should crum - ble _____ in the sea, _____

stand   by   me,   stand   by

me,   oh,   stand, _____   stand by

me.   If   the   me. _____

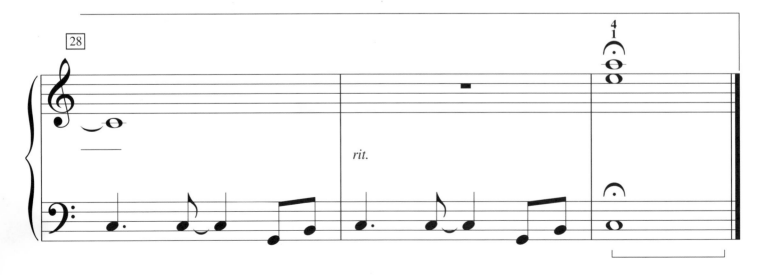

rit.

Tomorrow

from the Musical Production ANNIE

Lyric by Martin Charnin
Music by Charles Strouse
Arranged by Mona Rejino

Once Upon A Dream

from Walt Disney's SLEEPING BEAUTY

Words and Music by Sammy Fain and Jack Lawrence
Adapted from a Theme by Tchaikovsky
Arranged by Fred Kern

Accompaniment (Student plays one octave higher than written.)

eyes   is   so   fa - mil - iar   a   gleam. Yet, I

know   it's   true   that   vi - sions   are

sel - dom   all   they   seem.   But if

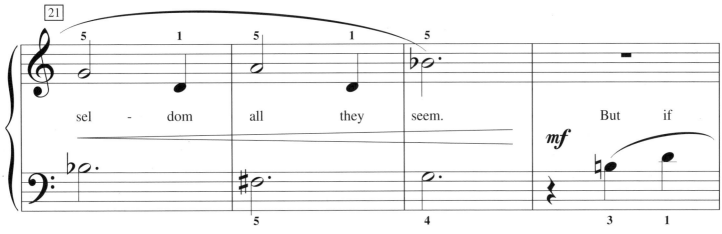

A Dream Is A Wish Your Heart Makes

from Walt Disney's CINDERELLA

Words and Music by Mack David,
Al Hoffman and Jerry Livingston
Arranged by Phillip Keveren

Accompaniment (Student plays one octave higher than written.)

With tenderness, in 'two' (♩ = 72)

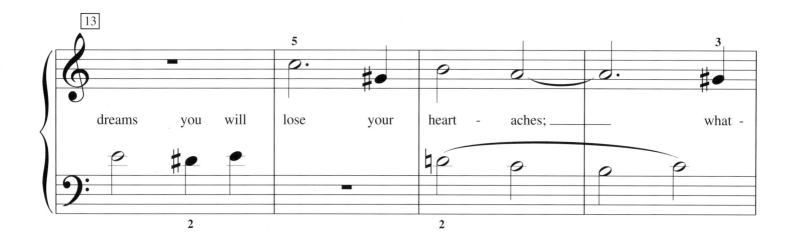

dreams you will   lose   your   heart - aches; _____ what -

ev - er you   wish   for, you   keep.   Have

mp

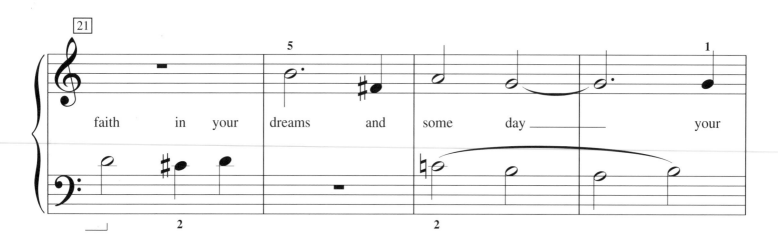

faith   in   your   dreams   and   some   day _____ your

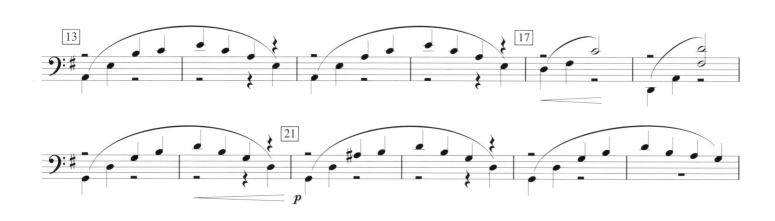

p

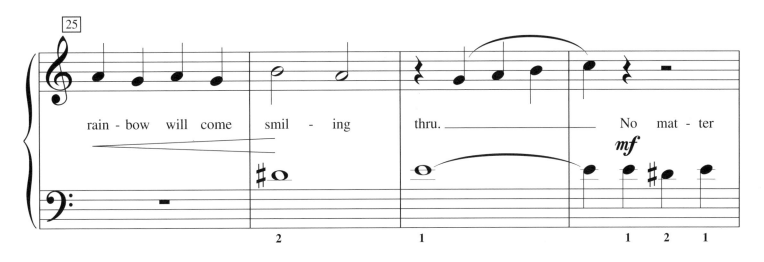

rain - bow will come smil - ing thru. No mat - ter

mf

how your heart is griev - ing, if you keep on be - liev - ing, the

dream that you wish will come true.

rit.

p

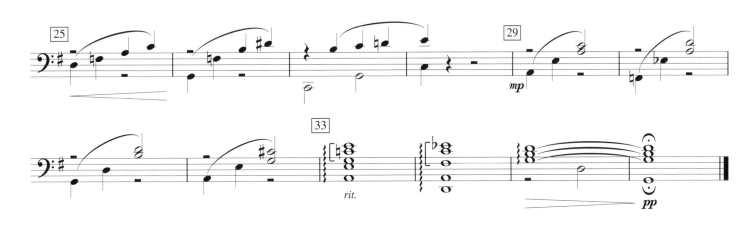

rit.

mp

pp

Go The Distance

from Walt Disney Pictures' HERCULES

Music by Alan Menken
Lyrics by David Zippel
Arranged by Phillip Keveren

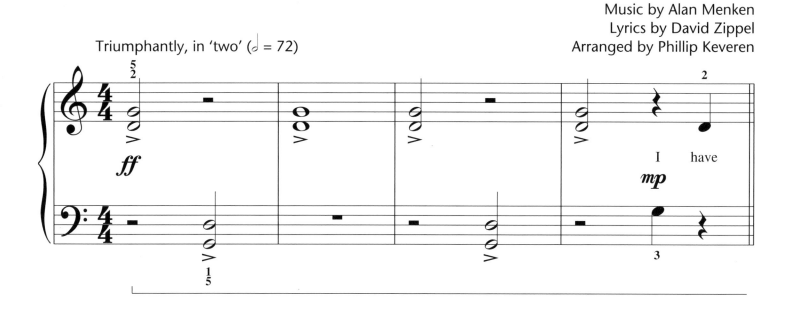

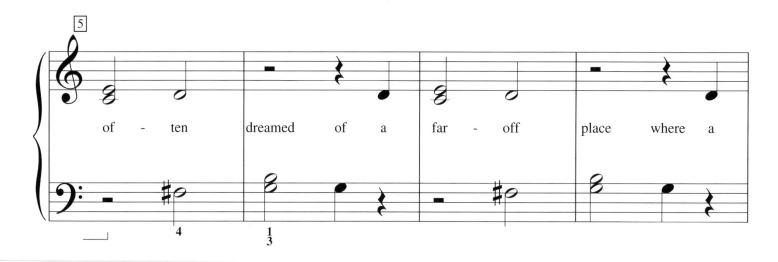

Accompaniment (Student plays one octave higher than written.)

Triumphantly, in 'two' (♩ = 72)

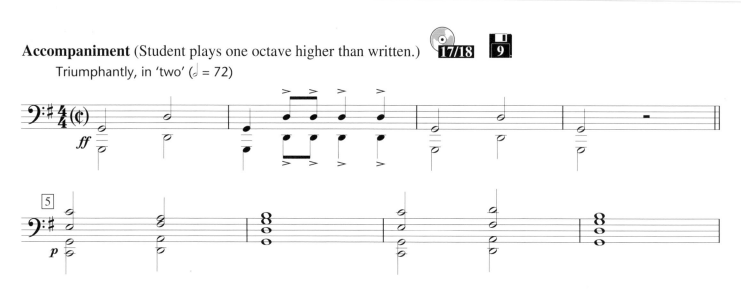

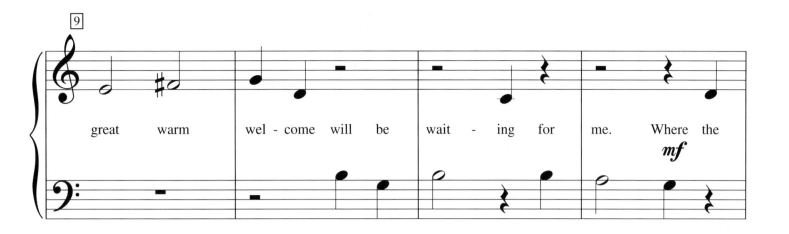

great warm wel - come will be wait - ing for me. Where the

crowds will cheer when they see my face, and a

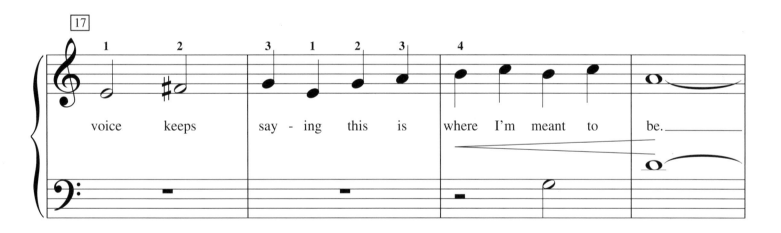

voice keeps say - ing this is where I'm meant to be.____

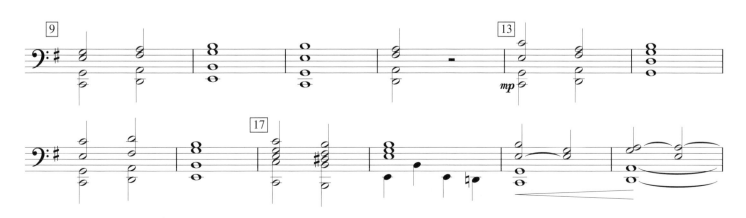

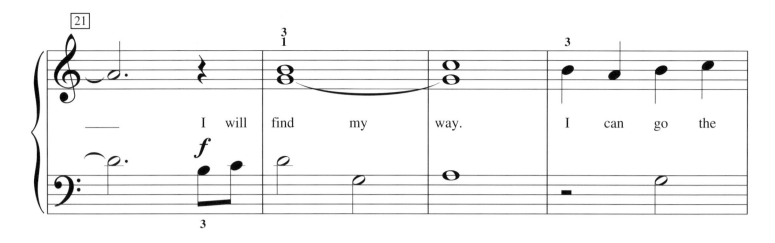

_____ I will find my way.   I can go the

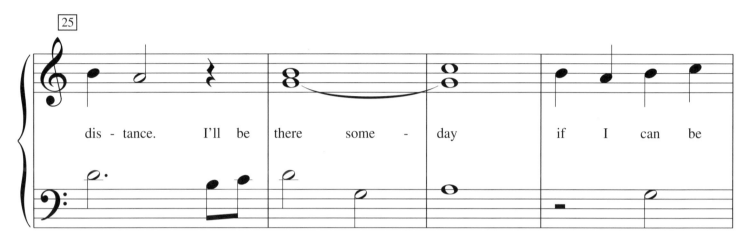

dis - tance.   I'll be there some - day   if I can be

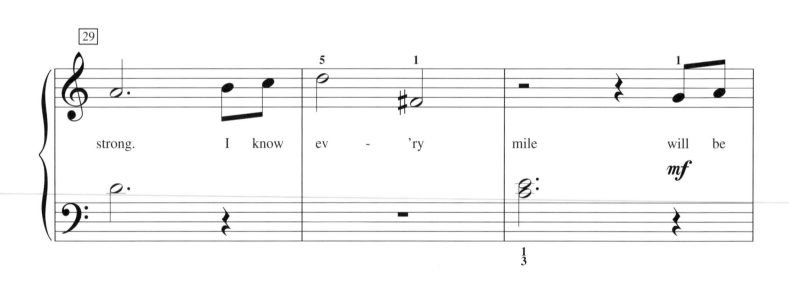

strong.   I know ev - 'ry mile   will be

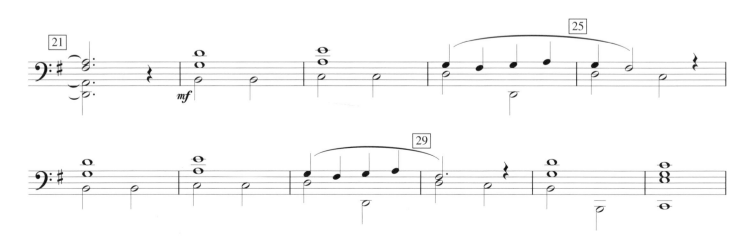

What A Wonderful World

Words and Music by George David Weiss
and Bob Thiele
Arranged by Mona Rejino